Girls Can Do Anything

Dedication

This book is dedicated to my daughters Makayla, Malia, and the numerous daughters I have adopted along the way. You are the future leaders of our communities. I am mindful of my responsibility to help create environments where anything is possible for you, if you believe and work towards your goals. You are beautiful and brilliant. Let your light shine so that the world can see who they can become if you put in the work and overcome the barriers. This path will not be easy **"No Grind No Glory".** I love you more than words can express. You have the ability to create whatever you will to be (**Ase'**).

To my wife, you are my heart and greatest supporter. Thank you for embodying greatness and class. My Queen, I super love you.
Shout out to my mom and sisters Lakeisha, Erica and Jenny. Also shout out to my sister from another mother L. Cable. Love you all to pieces. To my big little sister Keisha thank you for always having my back and for honest conversations when I need to make changes.

To Mrs. McDonald, thank you for being the inspiration for this book. You are an awesome example that you came become whatever you want when you put your mind to it and put in the work.

Ever since Jasmine first played with her first tablet, she loved technology. Jasmine wakes up early each morning so that she can play her favorite coding game before going to school. Sometimes, Jasmine is so into the game that she forgets to get dressed for school. Luckily, Jasmine's mom sets her alarm just in case Jasmine gets lost in her tablet.

Jasmine loves helping other students and her teacher when they have issues with the computers in class. Sometimes she gets teased by other students because when her teacher, Ms. Little, takes the class outside to play Jasmine often plays coding games while the other students are busy playing games.

While Jasmine is the classroom technology expert, there are times when Ms. Little has to call for the school tech support specialist to fix the laptop issues.

Whenever Mrs. McDonald comes in the room, Jasmine gets excited. Jasmine watches carefully as Mrs. McDonald fixes the laptop.

Sometimes, the children in Jasmine's classroom call her names like nerd, laptop-head, and Geek-Tron. Despite her teacher's interventions, students still make fun of Jasmine when the teacher is not looking.

The boys in the room often tease Jasmine telling her "Girls don't fix computers. Girls are models and do girl stuff." When Jasmine gets frustrated, she asks her teacher if she can go do her work in Mrs. McDonald's office.

Whenever Jasmine walks into Mrs. McDonald's office, she gives her a hug and has Jasmine help fix whatever laptop or computer in her office.

After a few minutes, Jasmine tells Mrs. McDonald why she is upset. Mrs. McDonald often reminds her that she can become whatever she wants to if she studies hard and puts in the work.

A few days a week, Mrs. McDonald and Jasmine eat lunch in the back of the library. During their lunch, Mrs. McDonald tells Jasmine stories of the challenge she experienced growing up being one little girl who loved fixing things. Mrs. McDonald explains, "when I was growing up in Southside Chicago we were so poor my brothers and sisters made cars and games from mattresses, furniture, and broken appliances.

Mrs. McDonald also had to deal with being teased because she loved to fix broken lamps and televisions. Her sisters and brothers often teased her when she went into their room taking wires from an old lamp and replacing it with the bad wires on broken lamps.

However, whenever someone had a problem with the appliances or televisions in the house, they took the broken items straight to her.

Jasmine often asked Mrs. McDonald how she dealt with being teased when she was younger. Mrs. McDonald told her, "I focused on the fun I had when I learned something new or when I fixed something broken around the house. I was ok with being different and I liked knowing that I could do special things with computers and appliances.

Mrs. McDonald told her stories about how sometimes her mother, step-dad and siblings would try to convince her to play with dolls or other girl related activities.

Despite not fitting in with her family's thoughts on what a girl should do, Mrs. McDonald understood that working as a waitress or being fine with staying at home while her husband worked somewhere in the city did not fit her vision for her life.

As time passed, girls in Jasmine's classroom saw how happy Jasmine was after meeting with Mrs. McDonald. Jasmine told them stories about how she learned how to fix computers and the coding games she played during her lunch sessions.

After hearing about all the fun Jasmine was having, the girls asked Mrs. McDonald if they could join her lunch group. Mrs. McDonald replied, "Yes, we always have room for another future scientist, engineer, and or CEO of a large corporation."

Knowing that planning the events for a large group of girls was going to be challenging, Mrs. McDonald asked the librarian, Dr. Smith, to help. Dr. Smith agreed to help.

Weekly, they met with the girls and explored various career paths and did STEM related activities. As staff members came to the library, they also offered to support the girls by donating funds and resources for fieldtrips. They also helped by having their various friends and sorority sisters come to the school and speak to the girls.

Not all of the girls' parents were excited about the girls learning about STEM careers and opportunities. Toya's mother believed that girls should be learning about hair and make-up related activities. Toya's mother eventually called up to the school to fuss at Mrs. McDonald about

her having her daughter in her group.
Mrs. McDonald invited Toya's mother to come up and join in the next girls group. Despite being reluctant about seeing the girls participate in the STEM related activities, she agreed to attend the next lunch group.

Toya's mother was amazed as she saw the girls replace parts on the various computers. She, like many women, were raised to think STEM was not for girls. After seeing the amazing job the girls did, Toya's mother, Ms. Jordan, apologized to Mrs. McDonald and promised to support the girls in any way she could. Periodically, Ms. Jordan would come to the girls group and help with the STEM activities.

As the word spread around the community about the amazing STEM group the girls were a part of, more and more business partners came to the school to support the girls. Eventually there were more than 50 girls in the group.

Mrs. McDonald enjoyed the ride as their small lunch group grew into something that would help build future female leaders.
Mrs. McDonald reminded Jasmine, "girls can do anything if they put their mind to it".

Reflections

Why were students teasing Jasmine?

What are some things you can do if you feel you are being picked on in school?

What are some careers in science, technology, engineering, and mathematics fields?

Why do some people think girls should not go into careers in science, technology, engineering, and mathematics fields?

If you were a parent would you support your daughter or son if they want to go into a career in science, technology, engineering, and mathematics fields?

STEM Organizations for Girls

Girls Who Code
https://girlswhocode.com

Girls In Tech
https://girlsintech.org

Black Girls Code
www.blackgirlscode.com

Girls Inc. | Inspiring All Girls to be Strong, Smart,
& Bold
https://girlsinc.org/

Society of Women Engineers
www.swe.org

Consider contacting following sororities chapters
regarding helping your school or organization with
having mentors or speakers come to speak/work with
your girls' group:

Alpha Kapa Alpha Sorority Inc.
Delta Sigma Theta
Zeta Phi Beta
Sigma Gamma Rho

Shadows of a Man

by Kenneth Vaughan
Illustrated by
Brittany Davis and Jasmine Lewis

Made in the USA
Monee, IL
21 September 2024